TRIBAL
TATTOO

Important Note
Body paint is for external use only

Warning
Any contact with the eyes should be avoided. However, if you do get paint in the eye, wash your eyes immediately
with cold water, or rinse with an eye bath. If symptoms persist then contact your doctor immediately.

THIS IS A CARLTON BOOK

First published in the USA by
Marlowe and Company
841 Broadway, 4th Floor
New York
NY 10003 ·

Text, book design and illustrations copyright © Carlton Books Limited, 2000

Library-of-Congress Cataloging-in-Publication Data available on request

ISBN 1 56924 610 6

Project Editor: Camilla MacWhannell
Art Editor: Adam Wright
Production: Janette Davis

Printed and bound in China

TRIBAL
TATTOO

ANDY SLOSS

Marlowe & Company

Contents

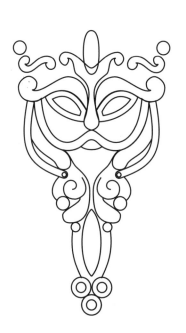

THE BODY BEAUTIFUL AND POWERFUL

Human beings are thought to be the only creatures who are conscious of themselves and their bodies as distinct from the outside world. The skin is the boundary between the exterior and interior worlds, the outward expression of our selves and the means by which we experience the outer world. Decorating this boundary has two opposite effects – it forms a bridge or path to allow the inner, spiritual self into the outside world, and it also reinforces the boundary, keeping the outer world out of the body. This is how tattooing has come to be used spiritually and as protection in cultures around the world.

Body art has a rich history, starting so far back in prehistory that we have no idea where or when it started, though it was probably before the invention of clothing. Unfortunately skin does not preserve well, but thousands of years before the first mummification, Stone Age rock paintings around the world depicted people with decorated bodies.

The Egyptians appear to have developed the art of tattooing in the Middle Kingdom (around 2000 BC), having learnt it from the Nubians to the south. A few mummified women have been found with patterns of tattooed dots or dashes on their bodies. The meanings of the patterns is unknown, but they all appear to have had some ritualistic purpose to do with the goddess Hathor. The most famous is the mummy of Amunet, a priestess of Hathor at Thebes.

Almost all societies that used tattooing did it using the same technique: a handle made from a straight stick or bone (preferably a jaw bone) with a line of thin hard bones (usually fish bones) or later on metal pins along it. These would be attached so that they all stuck out the same distance – just far enough to pierce the skin, but not far enough to do any serious damage to the person being tattooed. Then soot or ashes were rubbed into the wounds, so that when they healed the colour was trapped under the skin. Different societies made their ashes from different, culturally important, plants which would be burnt as a special part of the ritual of tattooing; having been burnt and crushed just before application, these ashes would have been virtually free from bacteria and similar. Tattooing was almost always first done as part of the initiation into adulthood, and the process could last from months to the entire life of the wearer, with more designs added to the body as more deeds needed to be recorded.

Tattooing a body by the traditional methods found around the world would have taken a long time to complete as not even the strongest warrior could survive so many (albeit small) wounds at one time. With few medicines to prevent infection, it is surprising that few died from infection or had their tattoos obscured or deformed by scarring, but it was a highly prized and specialized skill and those who practised it (usually priests) would have had generations of knowledge passed on to them before they were allowed to make their first tattoo.

In the last twenty years the popularity of the art of tattoo has exploded. Because of its origins in magic and social ranking amongst native tribes, European travellers and missionaries saw it as one of the ultimate signs of barbarity and did their utmost to eradicate it from the face of the earth and its people. But with increased contact with the people of the Pacific, and especially Japan, the Europeans could not deny the beauty and artistic merit of this ancient art form. First sailors took up the fashion, in the process developing a new language of designs, until the Navy actually made the suggestion that all sailors (even up to admirals) should be tattooed with the name of their ship at the very least, so as to help with identification of bodies after battles.

In the late nineteenth century attitudes had changed so radically that tattoos became the fashion at the top of British society. This did not last long, and by the early twentieth century tattoos were generally associated with sailors and carnival sideshow freaks. The return of tattooing as a popular art form in the West began in the 1960s when hippies and bikers started to get tattooed in order to mark themselves out as part of a group (or tribe) as well as usually proclaiming a message or belief that came from the core of the wearer (generally concerning peace and the freedom of the individual). And this is the way that it developed, so that now tattoos are used more than anything as a declaration of individuality. In an age when we can choose what we look like through surgery and cosmetics, trying to create the ultimate "body beautiful", many have chosen the opposite path where the body is made beautiful by becoming a canvas for their dreams and visions. For most, part of the reason for having a tattoo is as a rebellion against the modern plastic society, and in favour of a simpler, more honest and natural way of life, so the images used are taken from so-called "primitive" societies. They are often adapted and developed to suit modern sensibilities, with styles mixed in ways never seen before, and this is how the modern tribal style developed.

THE PACIFIC

Many Pacific cultures believe that artworks charge a person with power, both spiritually and socially. The decoration of the body, by tattoo or paint, acts like a lens for the internal spirit, reflecting and enhancing its power. The images can be used to attract the focus of the ancestors for added power, so that the body becomes the channel between the human and spirit worlds. Thus tattoos were used as a protective shell, as well as badges of social rank.

In parts of New Guinea there are older women who tattoo the young women during their transition to adulthood. Each tattoo is unique, a product of the spirit world channelled through the tattooist, though most have a vertical row of Vs down the middle of the forehead. As with the men, the tattoos are done to enhance the beauty of the women, but are also, due to the methods of tattooing used, signs of strength and endurance – the more tattoos you have, the stronger you must be.

Body paint, being temporary, does not have the power of tattoos, but was used for specific festivals. In New Guinea, for instance, the young Abelam men are richly painted and decorated for rituals, and through this they become (or become vessels for) the spirits of their ancestors. It is religious art, and they see body decoration as their greatest artistic achievement. As one artist said: "All those carved and painted objects are marvellous and holy. But the most marvellous and beautiful thing of all is a man with body decoration, adorned with flowers and feathers."

Although the styles and designs differ from one culture, one set of islands, to another, almost all of

them used large areas of solid black. This may have been an aspect of machismo, showing how much the wearer can take, but there were a lot of cultures whose men were tattooed with large rectangular blocks of solid black. One of the best-known variations on this was in Hawaii, where large areas of the body were tattooed with alternating triangles, diamonds or squares of tattoo and skin.

This was a far cry from the intricate designs that the Dutch mistook in Samoa for fine silk leggings. The currently popular Blackwork style comes from this tradition – simple designs made striking by the

contrast between solid black and flesh.

The styles varied from place to place and also changed over time. For example, the Maoris arrived in New Zealand towards the end of the first millennium AD as part of the ongoing migration from Polynesia. They brought with them the traditional culture, language, beliefs and art styles, including tattooing. Originally their designs were very similar to those of the other migrators, such as in Hawaii and the Cook Islands. But as time passed each group developed its own distinctive and unique styles.

Tattoos are known as *moko* to the Maori, and the highly skilled and revered artists who made them were known as *tohunga-ta-moko*. Most Pacific

tattooists made their designs by tapping a small toothed bone implement (a needle comb) with a wooden mallet and then rubbing soot into the wounds. The Maoris, on the other hand, used chisel-like implements. This led to, or was dictated by, the development of spiral designs, a major element of Maori art.

As in other cultures, tattoos were used as a mark of rank, so while body decoration was fairly common, the *moko* on the face were by far the most important. Slaves were not allowed tattoos, priests wore small patterns above the right eye, and women had few tattoos (apart from on the lips, which were tattooed to give them a more attractive bluish colour). Chiefs, nobles and female heads of families had their entire faces tattooed, a process that started at puberty and lasted several years. Every design was unique to its wearer, but could be copied on paper by the early European explorers, where they were used in place of signatures.

The abandonment of the straight, multi-toothed needle comb meant that curved line work took over from the mainly straight-line, geometric designs of their predecessors. The led to the development of the spiral patterns. These tended to be basic spirals, without the ever-more abstract variations that the Celts and others developed. This also meant that the designs could follow and emphasize the natural curves of the face and body in ways that had not been seen before. As mentioned earlier, it is this aspect of tattoo designs that distinguishes the very best of the modern tattooist's art.

One particular aspect of Maori art varies from the Blackwork style in a beautiful and delicate way.

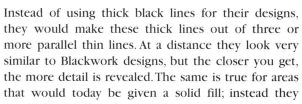

Instead of using thick black lines for their designs, they would make these thick lines out of three or more parallel thin lines. At a distance they look very similar to Blackwork designs, but the closer you get, the more detail is revealed. The same is true for areas that would today be given a solid fill; instead they would be filled with parallel, almost always curved, lines.

Adapting Blackwork designs to this style is simple. Once you have a Blackwork design that you are happy with, trace the outlines onto another sheet. Then put in a central line down the lines and curved parallel lines in all the areas. If the lines of the Blackwork design are wide, you can add more lines between the edges and the centre line to fill the space.

Unfortunately, the arrival of the Europeans did not just lead to the recording of tattoo styles and their development across the Pacific. It also heralded the arrival of Christian missionaries, who in the nineteenth century were particularly against tattooing. By the early twentieth century tattooing across much of the Pacific was a dying art. Then, with the independence movements, tattooing became a political statement. Today tattooing in the Pacific is often used as a means of affirming cultural identity and continuity of traditions, despite the encroachment of western religion and culture. Once again tattoos are a channel to the ancestors.

Polynesian tattoo designs range from semi-realistic images through the highly stylized to the totally abstract.

This is a tattoo which covered the head of a Polynesian man. The spirals were on the forehead.

The tattoos from the face of an Easter Island chief.

A Tongan sun symbol.

A pair of Maori monsters (*taniwha*).

15

Pacific

Maori repeat patterns taken from legbands.

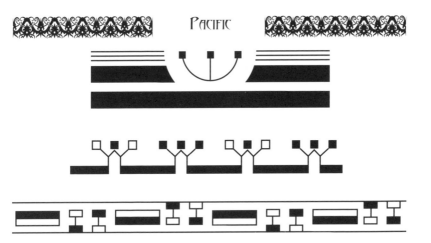

Tattoo designs in the Marquesas Islands developed from large, basic rectangular blocks to fine detailed work using only the most basic of geometrical shapes. This did not stop them from developing a diverse and unique range of images for armbands and legbands as well as individual designs.

17

The distinctive Sarawak designs of Borneo are unique in the world of tattooing, with their mix of symmetry and freehand expression. This led to them becoming the main original inspiration for modern Blackwork tattoo design, as to the modern eye they have timeless echoes of Art Nouveau, gothic art and the alien images of H.R. Giger.

The two designs above were used for armbands and legbands, while the freer, non-repeating design below could be placed anywhere on the body, depending on its scale.

SOUTH AMERICA

There is evidence that virtually all pre-Hispanic cultures in South America used tattoos or body painting. There were different techniques and a wide variety of styles, but they were all used for social or religious purposes, rather than purely for decoration. None of the societies had a written language, apart from the heiroglyphs of the Mayas and the Aztecs, so the images and colours that they used were part of a visual and spiritual language that is still not fully clear to us today. We do know that to the Aztecs and others in Central America four colours were of great importance, signifying points of the compass, gods and the quarters of every hour. Black was for Tezcatlipoca, the god of the North. Red was for Xipe Totec, the god of the East. Blue was for Huitzilopochtli, the god of the South. White was for Quetzalcoatl, the god of the West.

As an example of the complex and varying symbology of colours to the Aztecs, Tezcatlipoca was also the ruler of the four quarters of the day: when he was lord of the sunrise he was yellow, as lord of midday he was blue, as lord of the sunset he was red, and at night he was black. As you can see, yellow and white had very similar meanings to the Aztecs as they did to many tribes around the world.

To the Mayans these were the colours and directions of the four winds, who were followers of the rain god. So by colouring an image you can totally change its meaning, though the language of colour becomes increasingly convoluted as the society and its rituals become more rigid and stratified, and by inference, more decadent.

In a way the Aztecs were the last in this tradition; tattoos and body painting were seen as a channel for the gods and spirits of the ancestors, as with previous South American and other cultures. The images tended to be of humans and animals – presumably to form a spiritual link between the two – and even half-human, half-animal hybrids. The divine nature of the designs meant that they were not allowed for the rulers of the physical world, who had physical insignia of power – the throne and the robe.

The later Incas, however, merged religion and state and their rulers claimed descendancy from the gods, in particular the sun god, so tattoos became the symbol of both spiritual and secular power and solar images became commonplace. They also proscribed the use of images of the gods' creations, like many other cultures, so their art tended towards the geometrical. Because tattoos and body painting, and especially face painting, were used as a mark of rank, both socially and religiously, a whole graphical language developed, with exact rules for placement and colour of the designs, unfortunately all but lost to us now.

The rain forest tribes of hunter-gatherers virtually all used body paint for a wide variety of reasons. Some wore body paint in the same way as we wear clothes (and it was seen as shameful not to), others for camouflage, to invoke the spirits of animals or the ancestors, for religious events, or for purely decorative purposes.

The arrival of Cortez and the Spanish in 1519 heralded the end of most of the indigenous cultures, religions and art forms, including tattooing. The Spanish found a people who not only worshipped non-Christian idols, but had also found a way of permanently printing idolatrous images onto their bodies (tattooing had died out in Europe by this time). They did their utmost to wipe out tattooing and all other "satanic" practices, but when they found that even conversion to Christianity and baptism did not stop the natives from getting tattoos, they turned to torture, pillage and genocide, proudly destroying all that they could find of these ancient civilizations.

Unfortunately this means that the best descriptions of the Central American art of tattooing come from those who set out to eradicate it. From these we know that the more tattoos you had, the braver and stronger you were considered, while people who had no tattoos were mocked and scorned. Men and women were both tattooed, with women being tattooed from the waist up in designs that were more delicate than those of the men.

Pictorial images of tattoos that remain are limited to incised statues, some pottery and the heiroglyphics of the Incas. But the designs have not all been lost because they used a technique found nowhere else in the world. To transfer the design to the skin before tattooing it they used the same pottery stamp blocks that they used for printing on their fabrics. Many of these have been found, giving us direct access to the later patterns used, including cylinders with raised patterns on them that could be rolled across the skin to produce a continuous band for armbands and legbands. Most of the designs in this chapter are taken from these stamp blocks.

The Aztecs had a distinctive abstract geometrical style, the product of centuries of development, that look very modern to us.

Sun symbols were very popular because of their links to the king, who was seen as an incarnation of the sun god.

24

25

Repeat patterns of all kinds were used as tattooed and painted armbands, legbands and even printed on pottery and cloth using cylindrical stamps.

27

NORTH AMERICA

There were thousands of different tribes in North America before the arrival of the Europeans, each with their own cultures and artistic language. Tattooing and body painting for special occasions appear to have been important to virtually all of them. The term "redskin" comes from the prevalence of body painting, especially amongst the Plains tribes. Unlike most of the other cultures described in this book, their use was less for social and spiritual power, and more to do with individual prowess, beauty and respect. Not to be tattooed was a disgrace, but to falsely wear a tattoo was even worse – the offending tattoo would have to be publicly cut off, a punishment that could often be fatal. Different methods for applying tattoos were also used in North America, though not widely: such as the "scratching" technique, where the design is drawn in soot on the body, the skin is scratched and the soot rubbed into the wounds; or the "thread" method, where a thread covered with soot is passed through the skin to create straight tattoo lines.

Because the Native Americans died out so quickly due to new diseases and weapons, and the Europeans of the time were not interested in tattoo and body art styles, almost all evidence of the art has now been lost. From brief comments and journal entries by early explorers and missionaries, it would appear that almost all of the native tribes of North America used to tattoo themselves to some extent, but that is almost all we know. Another problem is that many early observers made no differentiation between tattooing and body painting, so much of what is described as tattoo was, if fact, body and face painting, especially when colour is mentioned, as almost all tattooing was black (with a few tribes using red as well). The following comes from the few contemporary writings and drawings that were made on the subject.

As well as the usual social and spiritual meanings, various tribes used tattoo for a wide range of reasons. Many used it for medicinal reasons, such as the Ojibwa, who tattooed the cheeks and foreheads of those suffering chronic toothache or headaches. The practice of tattooing brave warriors was taken a step further by depicting the battles on the warrior himself, so his body became a catalogue of his deeds, for all to marvel at. An Iroquois chief had 60 symbols tattooed on his thighs, one for each enemy he had killed, like modern-day fighter pilots marking their planes. The inhabitants of Virginia and Florida, according to a sixteenth century explorer, had their "hands, legs, breasts and faces cunningly embroidered with diverse marks, such as beasts and serpents, artificially wrought into their flesh with black dots".

The only serious study of tribal tattoos among the Native Americans was undertaken by James Swan in the late nineteenth century in the northwest. According to him almost all the tribes of the northwest used tattoos, but the greatest artists were the Haida. They used their tattoos like coats of arms, denoting their family name and spirit – bear, beaver, wolf, eagle, fish. To them every part of a design, including the colours used (mainly pale shades) held meaning, and they covered more of the body than any of their neighbours. The men were tattooed between their shoulder blades, on their chests, on the front of their thighs and on the legs and feet from the knee down. The women were tattooed on their chests, shoulders, from the knees down and from the elbows down over the backs of the hands. Swan was told that he ought to have a swan tattoo, so that they would know his name.

Another northwest tribe, the Kwakiutl, developed a style of animal designs that has become very popular in the last ten years for tattoos, but while they use this style for painting buildings, on totem poles, and so on, there is no direct evidence that they ever tattooed in this style. Their tattoos used large areas of solid black and thick stripes to make even more highly stylized representations of animals, and unlike the Haida they favoured strong colours and bold shapes, with little intricacy.

They were one of the very few tribes in the world who were not limited to tattooing in black. For many of their designs they filled in the black outlines with a red body, not only making them more dramatic and visible, but also embuing them with more symbolic power, red being the colour for blood and the life-force.

Because of the wealth of natural resources the tribes of the northwest were the most wealthy of all the North American tribes, so it is odd that despite using virtually identical techniques to tribal tattooists the world over, the mortality rate from infection in the northern tribes seems to have been higher than normal. This was probably due to the harshness of life in general, but it did make tattooing a riskier, and therefore more potent and prestigious, ritual. Both tattooist and subject were seen to have proven themselves worthy to the spirit whose image was depicted.

At festivals and rituals, painted masks were used by almost all these tribes, but from the few contemporary pictures it appears that the styles used were markedly different from the facial tattoos that were worn. Being a large part of what remains of the artistic cultures, they are still worth looking at for inspiration.

Meanwhile, on the opposite coast the Algonquin-speaking tribes used a much more delicate, geometric style, more decorative and less representative. They went in for armbands, legbands and "necklaces" and patterns that covered enough of the body to confuse early Europeans into thinking that they were fully clothed. And it was not just styles that varied from tribe to tribe, area to area, but the meaning of the symbols and colours too.

For instance the Cherokees thought white signified happiness and black signified death, but to many others black was the symbol for happiness, and white was used for mourning and communication with the ancestors. Almost always red was the colour for war, success and victory. These meanings were not fixed, however, and could change at specific times and for certain rituals.

One design that was found in body painting throughout North America, regardless of tribe and tradition, was the hand print, usually on the face. This was almost certainly due to the fact that body and face painting was done by the wearers themselves, using a bowl of water as a mirror, so patterns and designs were only applied where they could be seen and reached by the wearer. A handprint on the face to finish off the work would have been a mark of the individual, not unlike the signature at the bottom of a painting.

Two contrasting sun symbols

Tattooed armbands, representing the real armbands worn by several Plains tribes, with stylized feathers hanging from them, were common.

Animal images were used – as in every other part of the world – to protect hunters from the predators depicted, or to give them the strength or skills of the animal and its spirit.

34

Images of people tended to be painted as they were used for special occasions and ceremonies. The one notable exception was in the tribes who used tattoos to record the important events (hunts, battles and so on) in the wearer's life. A great hunter-warrior could expect to be covered with images of his exploits by the time of his death.

35

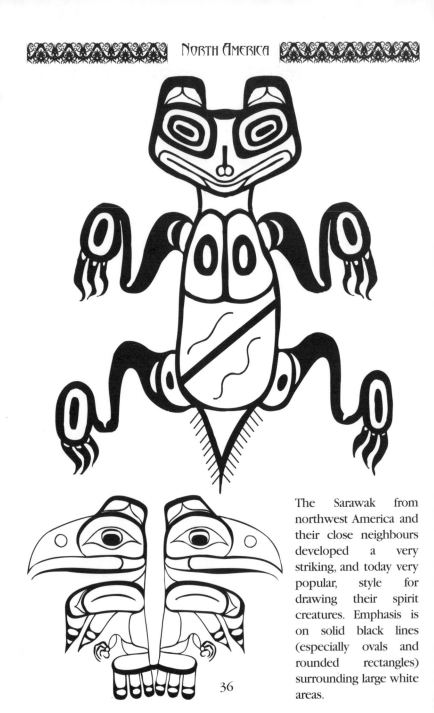

The Sarawak from northwest America and their close neighbours developed a very striking, and today very popular, style for drawing their spirit creatures. Emphasis is on solid black lines (especially ovals and rounded rectangles) surrounding large white areas.

36

THE PAINTED PEOPLE OF EUROPE

Tattooing in Europe has a long history that probably stretches back to the earliest Siberian nomads. They, in turn, may well have learned the art from much further south. That it travelled through, and was practised in, the Middle East is show by the prohibitions against tattooing (defiling God's creation) in both Muslim and Jewish law. Thracian women were tattooed and though the ancient Greeks used tattooing mainly for marking slaves and criminals, occasionally young nobles would have themselves tattooed to show their bravery. The Romans did not originally tattoo themselves, but as their empire invaded the surrounding cultures that did, tattooing was taken up. However, the practice was banned by Emperor Constantine, when the Roman Empire became officially Christian, for being barbaric and pagan. Unfortunately, little or no evidence remains to show us what designs these early societies used for their tattoos.

So far no physical evidence has come to light to prove that the Celts (continental or insular) used tattoos decoratively or for ritual purposes. Several of the better preserved bodies found in bogs and similar on the continent can be seen to have short lines or sets of lines tattooed on their bodies, but it was not until the discovery of "Ötzi", the 5,400-year-old man found frozen in the Alps that the first clues were found as to their purpose. The marks on his feet and on his back correlate very closely with the acupuncture points used to treat rheumatism and arthritis, which he suffered from. Presumably the points were tattooed to heal the person or so that others could find them for repeated treatments - a sort of easily readable

prescription. This means that although the Celts knew the techniques for tattooing, it was in the hands of the healers rather than the artists.

The only reference to Celtic tattooing is from St Isadore of Seville in the sixth century AD where he says that the people of northern Britain:

> *incise on their bodies coloured pictures of animals, of which they are very proud. The Scots derive their name in their own language (Prytani) from their painted bodies, because these are marked with various designs by being pricked with iron needles with ink on them. The Picts (from the Latin, meaning "painted") are also thus named because of the absurd marks produced on their bodies by craftsmen with tiny pinpricks and juice extracted from local plants.*

While this seems to be a perfect description of the art of tattooing, it cannot be verified as there is no other evidence to be found anywhere.

But while tattooing was an apparently unknown art to the Celts of the British Isles, they made up for this with body painting. In the first century BC, the historian Herodian wrote: "They mark their bodies with various figures of all kinds of animals and wear no clothes for fear of concealing these figures." Caesar later added: "All the Britons dye their bodies with woad, which achieves a blue colour, and shave the whole of their bodies except the head and the upper lip" (presumably to make painting easier).

The Latin word that is translated as "woad" is found nowhere else in Roman literature, and experts

now doubt whether woad was actually used. Copper-based pigments have been suggested, but there is documentary evidence that the Celts used to produce dyes of all shades from red through purple to blue from one plant – madder. Because this was the a way to produce imperial purple (a very valuable colour to the Romans), the techniques were kept very secret and are lost to us today.

Herodian, in the third century AD, said: "They paint their bodies with sundry colours, with all kinds of animals represented in them." From this and their obvious love of, and skill with, colour (as can be seen in the great Christian illuminated manuscripts) it seems safe to assume that woad was not the only dye that the Celts used. There are innumerable vegetable and mineral dyes that the Celts had knowledge of and it is very likely that the flamboyant Celts would have used all the colours at their disposal to impress or terrify.

Even though the Celtic scribes tended to use as many colours as they could lay their hands on, even the most complex knotwork border would never have more than four colours, and one of these was used as a contrasting background colour. Even when the range of available colours was small, such as in the Lichfield Gospels, the scribes put them to very good effect.

They used strong contrasts wherever possible so that, when viewed at a distance where the detail is lost, the colours make a pattern of their own. Often this was done by simply using light and dark colours set against each other.

Unlike so much prehistoric art, many of their designs, such as animal designs, are well recorded. The Bibles that the Celtic scribes copied from were Byzantine and had no such animal images, so they

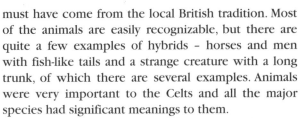

must have come from the local British tradition. Most of the animals are easily recognizable, but there are quite a few examples of hybrids – horses and men with fish-like tails and a strange creature with a long trunk, of which there are several examples. Animals were very important to the Celts and all the major species had significant meanings to them.

The intricate knotwork patterns of the later Christian period are the most popular of the different Celtic styles in tattooing today. This is because the geometry is straightforward and relatively easy to learn, while being adaptable to virtually any shape or space. Knotwork bands are very popular as armbands, especially the simple two-strand interlace. There is not room here to explain how to draw knotwork, but there are quite a few "teach yourself" books on the subject.

The early Celts were experts at decorating spirals and circular designs in ways found nowhere else in the world. This led to the development of a very fluid style that had echoes in the Art Nouveau movement two thousand years later. When they engraved these patterns onto bronze they showed the sense of balance between design and background that distinguishes the best Blackwork artists of today.

Despite having trading contacts with civilizations all along the north Atlantic and Mediterranean coasts, and having copied styles from all over, it was only really with the arrival of the Romans and Christians that the Celts developed the geometric art styles for which they and the Book of Kells are rightly famous. Their genius was not in the invention of new styles, like some other cultures, but in their ability to adapt and develop the styles they came across and turn them into something that was uniquely Celtic.

The Celts were masters of the spiral, with more variations than any other culture over a period of three thousand years.

41

The later years of Celtic culture in Britain, when the Picts reached the peak of their power, saw an explosion in the development in animal images.

42

Celtic art is famous for its knotwork, spiral and otherwise.

Knotwork bands make very popular armband designs.

43

45

Pictish symbols tended to be of important animals, both real and fantastical. The curled patterns on the boar's side were used for most four-legged animals to signify the shoulders and hips, becoming more and more abstract over a thousand years.

AFRICA – LAND OF RICH COLOURS

The traditional method of tattoo, of marking out designs with black dots, works less well as the skin darkens. For this reason if no other, tattooing does not have a rich tribal history in central and southern Africa. The equivalent marking of patterns is generally done either by scarification (which makes the designs more visible by making them three-dimensional) or by painting. And in this the African societies excel all others. In some tribes every adult has his or her "make-up kit" with powdered paints and fat for applying it. The sheer range of styles and patterns, the meanings of the images and their colours is overwhelming.

Luckily for us Africa proved more resilient to genocide and conversion than most of the continents invaded by the Europeans, so many of the traditional styles and their meanings have not been lost. But strangely, considering the wealth of history and the wide range of body painting designs all across the continent, there has been very little study into them and their meanings.

Some designs are obvious, like the painting of spots all over the body, while others are more symbolic, such as lines on the legs or forehead to represent fast or horned animals. A lot are purely decorative, things of beauty or expressions of the wearer's mood.

Because it is painless and relatively quick to apply, body paint designs tend to be bigger than their tattoo equivalents, covering large areas with solid colours, but without the overtones of strength and endurance. Colour is used far more widely and to greater effect than in any traditional tattoo style. Traditionally, as in many parts of the world, only three colours were used for body painting - black, made up from soot and charcoal; white, made from ashes or clay; and red, from red ochre (ofter baked in a special ritual to make it redder).

White is usually used to create a dramatic contrast, as black tattoos are against white skin. But white as a colour had a special significance for many African tribes - it symbolizes the link between this world and the spirit world of the ancestors or other, not necessarily friendly, spirits. It was therefore often used in initiation ceremonies when a child becomes an adult with access to the spirit world. It also symbolized purity and so had healing and protective elements.

White was often used with another colour or colours to bring out the contrasts and conflicts between the colours and their meanings. Red also held a wealth of meanings, depending where and when it was used. Being the colour of blood, to some it symbolized pain, war and death, while others saw it as health, happiness and life.

Who could use which colours and when were subject to strict social rules. A Nuba boy, for instance, was allowed to wear white and red from about eight, yellow when he became a young man and finally black when he was initiated. Excavations in the ancient Nubian city of Aksha uncovered mummies of women with tattoo patterns that were identical to those found on the Egyptian mummified priestesses of Hathor, so it is assumed that the Egyptians learnt the art from a people who are now masters of body painting.

Animal images have become increasingly stylized over thousands of years of use. They are worn as tattoos or painted to give the wearer either the power of the animal or protection from it.

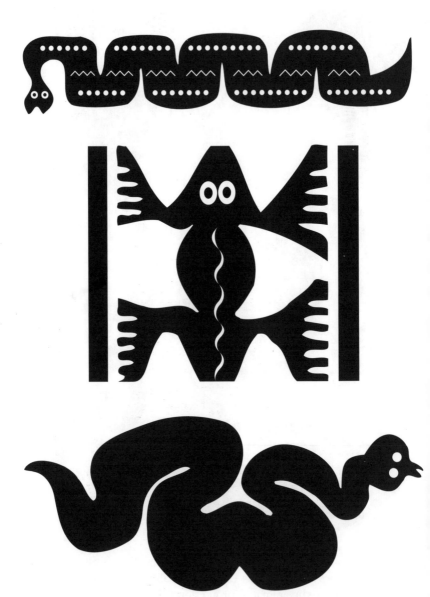

51

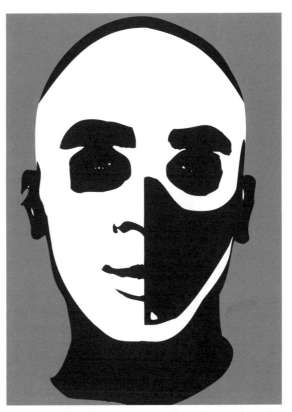

Most tribes in Africa paint their faces white for celebrations, festivals and rituals, leaving part or parts unpainted. The contrast between black and white shapes makes for some very striking designs.

Another common method for body painting is to paint the limbs or the whole body white and then, with fingers or sticks, remove the white in flowing lines, using the fingers, or any shape the artist wants, using an implement. The design on the right was made using four fingers to remove paint from the wearer's leg.

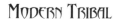

MODERN TRIBAL

In the last twenty years a new style has developed in the world of tattoo: Tribal tattoo. Although it originated in the traditional designs of tribes all around the world, it has now grown into a formal style in its own right. Today "Tribal" describes a specific style of tattoo in the same way that "Primitive" art is not at all the same thing as primitive art, despite being rooted in it.

Modern tribal styles can be traced back to the opening up of Japan in 1872. Japan had a tradition of tattoo as art, which the people of Europe had not seen before. This started the change in attitudes of the Church and public that has led to its current acceptance.

The current resurgence in the art of tattooing over the last twenty years in fact started in the early 1960s when a small number of American tattooists, including Cliff Raven and Leo Zulueta, turned away from the brightly coloured pictorial tattoos that had been the fashion and started to look towards the original tattoos of the Pacific islanders. Photographs of these tattoos in books and magazines spread the word and soon people who would not have considered having "Mother" or the like on their arm before were proudly displaying Blackwork designs that defied description. The more visible they became, the more popular the art of tattooing became, and for the first time in generations it was seen as an art form rather than merely a craft or the most outward sign of barbarity. This led trained artists into the field, which in turn helped change public perception further, so that now it is not unusual to think of a tattoo as

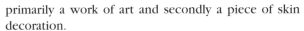

primarily a work of art and secondly a piece of skin decoration.

One of the benefits of the acceptance of tattoos as art and the fashion for tribal tattoos has been the rediscovery of the tattoos and their meanings and importance in the places they came from. As prejudice against tattooing dies, more and more cultures are discovering their tattoo heritage. The cultural historians may be trying to discover the development of the art and its main themes, but the natives are using it to show their strength and independent cultures and to remake contact with their ancestors.

Blackwork is a striking style that developed from various Pacific styles, but now covers almost all abstract and non-representational styles. As its name suggests, only black is used, and the designs get their power from the contrast between solid black and a pale skin. Blackwork designs tend to be simple, stark and graceful, and because black tattoo ink is the most stable, the edges look sharp for longer.

The most important consideration when designing an abstract tattoo is that it should flow with the body or highlight an aspect of the body. The body is a mobile, stretchable, three-dimensional object, so a design that works on paper will not always work on the body. A tattoo can make you look taller or shorter, rounder or thinner, or just highlight a good feature. Or you can use it as a sort of jewellery, for instance an armband of traditional Celtic knotwork or Native American feathers. Like an expensive piece of clothing (after all you will be wearing it all the time), it should flatter you and draw other people's attention.

If you really want to impress you could go for one of the traditional Japanese designs that cover large areas of the body with one unified image, usually using the subtle shading that is associated with watercolours. They tend to cover the whole of the back, one side of the front of the body or one whole arm – all of which tend to spread and fade onto the adjacent parts of the body, rather than stopping abruptly and artificially marking the edge of a body part. Incidentally this is one of the major advantages of the Blackwork style: that several different designs on different parts of the body can work together through their similar style to give the impression of a single overall design, in contrast to representational tattoos, which can end up forming a disturbing patchwork of different styles, colours and scales.

This does not tend to happen with Blackwork designs, because no matter how wide a range, historically and geographically, of styles used for different tattoos the reliance on strong contrasts and emphasis on form means that they will almost certainly complement each other. Almost all abstract styles and influences have been used for inspiration – from Celtic manuscripts through Mucha to Miro and beyond. It all depends on how you want to express yourself.

A few basic guidelines for drawing Blackwork designs:

- a bold shape is needed, with a balance between tattoo and skin – the areas of skin enclosed by the tattoo are as important as the tattoo itself;
- as well as a bold overall shape, a design should have fine detail so that it continues to attract the eye at different scales, like fractal images – hooks,

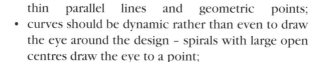

thin   parallel   lines   and   geometric   points;
- curves should be dynamic rather than even to draw the eye around the design – spirals with large open centres draw the eye to a point;

Dynamic   Even

- it is always worthwhile to see what a design will look like repeated as a reflection – a piece of . mirror with little or no frame can quickly give you an idea of whether it is worth drawing out.

And remember, a true Blackwork design should be like a Rorschach inkblot with no obvious representation but a world of possibilities.

And what about colour? There is only one rule about colour, which is that all rules are made to be broken sometimes. And in the last few decades the colour range and stability of tattoo inks has improved enormously so there is very little that can not be done. If you can draw it, it can almost certainly be tattooed, as long as the tattoo artist is able and willing. This has led to a growth in the last few years in tattoos in the style of modern "tribes" such as spraycan graffiti lettering and hip-hop cartoons where brilliant colour combinations can be used that reflect a more "pop" colour sense.

Anything is possible as long as you can find a tattoo artist who is up to the job.

59

62

MAKING YOUR OWN DESIGNS

The first thing to say is the most obvious: do not try to tattoo yourself. Even though you won't kill yourself, probably, you will be giving yourself an ugly, messy and embarrassing collection of scar tissue to remind you just how stupid a mistake can be for the rest of your life.

On the other hand designing a tattoo to be put on professionally can be a deeply spiritual and self-affirming exercise.

The first thing to do is to decide where on your body you want the tattoo. Different designs work better on different parts – a Blackwork design needs to be fairly large and visible from a distance to achieve full impact, so would not usually work as a small design on the ankle, for instance. Similarly a small design would look lost in the middle of an undecorated back.

Having chosen the position and scale for your design the next step is to choose the style. I have tried to show as wide a range of styles as possible in this book, but as the subject is so huge, I have only just managed to scratch the surface. Once you know the style it is a very good idea to look for more examples in your local library. You can try searching the Web, but for images libraries tend to be better, except for the Blackwork style, which is so new that there are very few books on the subject yet.

And when it comes to colours, you can do whatever you want. Up to the last thirty years, tattoo dyes were not very stable, and tended to fade and bleed (spread out), leaving a washed-out memory of the original after a few years, but this is no longer the case. Of course if you want it to look like a traditional

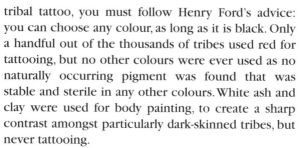

tribal tattoo, you must follow Henry Ford's advice: you can choose any colour, as long as it is black. Only a handful out of the thousands of tribes used red for tattooing, but no other colours were ever used as no naturally occurring pigment was found that was stable and sterile in any other colours. White ash and clay were used for body painting, to create a sharp contrast amongst particularly dark-skinned tribes, but never tattooing.

Next comes the hard or fun part, depending on your talents: the drawing of the design. You have access to tools that tribal tattooists couldn't even dream of – tracing paper, photocopiers, computers – all of which can help with your design.

Once you have a design that you are happy with it is always a good idea to put it away out of sight for a while – the longer the better, so that you can come back to it with a changed perspective. If you do not like it as much, see if you can see why and then play around with it until it looks better. This is often done by changing just one line: thinning or thickening it, changing the curve, or similar, is enough to change the balance and dynamic of the entire design.

Now, just to test your resolve – remember a tattoo is for life, not just a party – make a fake tattoo version of it to show trusted friends for a day or two. This technique can be used to transfer complicated designs to the skin. These can then be filled in with any type of body paint.

If you are still happy with it take a copy of the design down to the best tattooist in town (or one whose work you have seen and admired). And do it.

Create and enjoy.

BODY PAINTING

All of the techniques and materials listed below are designed to be safe to apply to the skin, but every person is different and some may develop an allergic reaction to some paints or dyes. When trying new paints, or painting a new person, always test for a reaction by applying a small amount of the paint to the inside of the elbow and leaving it for an hour or so. If there is no reaction – and there almost never will be – then it should be safe to cover larger areas with the paint.

In this chapter we will be covering body paint, which is temporary and can be cleaned off, rather than dyes which stain the skin and so last much longer. Theatrical make-up such as cake make-up is not covered as it is harder to apply and remove and easier to smudge in normal use. If you are painting these designs for theatrical or film use, a theatrical make-up manual should be consulted.

FAKE TATTOOS
If you want to make a temporary tattoo, there are two fairly simple methods.

First, using a dark blue or black ballpoint pen, copy your design (in reverse if you want it a particular way round) onto the smoothest, shiniest paper you have. Waxed paper is the best as you can trace the design through it, but ballpoint pens tend not to work well on it. Then place the design face down on the body and rub it from behind with cotton wool dipped in acetone (nail polish remover). This will make the ink transfer to the skin. If the ballpoint pen does not work on your chosen paper, you can use a felt pen, but the image will be much fainter and less sharp.

With the outline marked you can now fill in the areas with colour. For a temporary tattoo that is quick and easy to wash off, the easiest things to use are children's felt-tip pens. Being translucent, they do not obscure the surface of the skin like paints, but let it show through like real tattoos. Because of the area that will need to be covered, the broader the nib of the pen the better. The best are chisel-tipped pens as they can be used for fine lines as well as filling in areas.

These designs are easy to wash off with soap and water, but as the inks are soluble they should only be used when there will not be any water or sweat to make them run and fade.

BRUSHES

For these designs it is best to have four brushes: one thin round brush for fine detail and touching up any smudged areas, one medium round brush for the outlines, one medium flat brush for filling in areas and for painting lines that vary in width (for a pen-like line), and, one large round brush for filling in large areas of colour.

All these brushes should be as soft as possible so as not to irritate the skin. Soft brushes also hold the paint better, make smoother, more even lines and are easier to clean. Sable and squirrel (artificial if possible) are the best. After use they should be cleaned in warm, soapy (not detergent) water, unless the instructions on the paint ask for special cleaning requirements, and kept in a jar with the bristles upwards, so that they do not bend.

When painting always remember to rinse the brushes in clean, warm water between different colours or they will become "muddy".

Always try to draw lines on one smooth stroke,

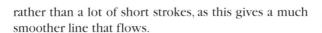

rather than a lot of short strokes, as this gives a much smoother line that flows.

FACE PAINTS

The most obvious choice of paints are water-soluble face paints because they are relatively cheap and designed to be painted on children, and so are as non-toxic as possible. They are available from most large toy shops and department stores and come in small palettes or individual pots. They are easy to apply and dry quickly. Some brands smudge much more easily than others (it depends on the amount of grease in the paints) so it is worth experimenting to find the best available locally.

Face paints come in a wide range of bright colours and are opaque.

TEXTILE ACRYLICS

These are actually designed for airbrushing on cloth, but they seem to work well on skin and are non-toxic. They dry quickly and don't rub off easily. Because they are made for textiles they are not as prone to cracking and peeling in the way that ordinary acrylics do. Yet they still wash off easily in soap and water. While they are designed for airbrushing, they still work well with brushes. Airbrushing is useful for smooth shading, especially over large areas or when using stencils.

CLEANING UP

Cold cream and cosmetic cleansers are the best things for removing water-based as well as oil-based paints. Baby wipes can also be very effective at removing water-based paints.

Smooth a layer of cold cream over the design, leave it for a minute and then gently rub it off with

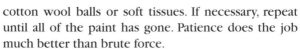

cotton wool balls or soft tissues. If necessary, repeat until all of the paint has gone. Patience does the job much better than brute force.

If you get paint on your clothes wash it out with cold water followed by detergent if it is water-based. If it is oil-based the detergent should be used first.

PAINTING

Having chosen your design and drawn it to the scale you want it you can trace it onto a piece of waxed paper, using a thin dark felt-tip pen. The lines will only be patchy but will be useable as a guide. Another method you can use is to put the sheet with your design on something soft (a piece of cotton or several sheets of waste paper) and prick holes with a pin along all the lines. Place it on the skin and rub the design with a sponge dipped in paint. This will give you a dotted outline to follow.

The second step is to fill in the areas with the colours of your choice, painting up to the outline that you marked. So as not to smudge the parts that are already painted, do not rest your hand on the skin when painting. Next you paint in the outline in a darker colour, painting it so that the line is as smooth as possible. The centre of the line should follow the edge of the area that you previously painted, so that half is on paint and half on skin. The reason for doing the outline last is so that it is an even width throughout.

STENCILLING

Stencilling is suitable for covering large areas with a repeated pattern, or if you want to paint several people with the same design. It also allows you to create subtler and more creative shading and when airbrushed in several colours designs look very impressive.

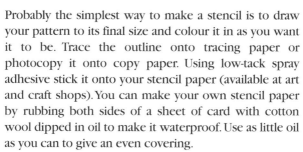

Probably the simplest way to make a stencil is to draw your pattern to its final size and colour it in as you want it to be. Trace the outline onto tracing paper or photocopy it onto copy paper. Using low-tack spray adhesive stick it onto your stencil paper (available at art and craft shops). You can make your own stencil paper by rubbing both sides of a sheet of card with cotton wool dipped in oil to make it waterproof. Use as little oil as you can to give an even covering.

Referring to your coloured version, cut out all the pieces of one colour, cutting through both the copy and the stencil. Carefully unpeel the copy from the stencil and stick it to a second stencil. Cut out all the pieces of the second colour, and so on for each of the colours you have chosen.

You can stick the stencils to the skin using the same spray adhesive. Then, using an airbrush, stencilling brush, sponge or cotton wool ball, apply the paint. Repeat this with each of your stencils, taking care to align the different colours as well as you can. When you have finished you can add an outline with a brush, or any other decoration you want.

A final note on colours: on Caucasian skin, black is always used for most outlines to give the design enough contrast to stand out, nothing else gives the dramatic impact that suits tattoos. Red is the second most used colour because of its strength – red attracts the eye more than any other colour. Blue tends often to be used as a form of shading and softening of the black outline on the inside of the design, while the outside edge is still sharp black. Greens and purples tend to be only used to colour in pictures, as on their own they are associated with bruising and ill-health. Yellow is even more rarely used as it not only looks sick and jaundiced, but also does not stand out on white skin.

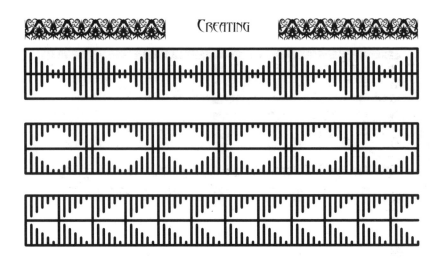

Many tribes used variations on simple geometric shapes, repeating them to make armbands and legbands. Often several bands would be put next to each other to create a much thicker band, usually with a complicated design being used for the top and bottom bands, with simpler designs in between.

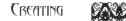

The number of variations on a simple band of triangles and circles is infinite, but when you are designing an armband made up of simple strips it is best to keep a common theme or themes in all of them. Elements such as line thickness, ratio of black to white, repeating exactly the same shapes with a different filling in each, the ratio of straight lines to curves and so on, all help to hold the design together.

Because the body is curved rather than angular many Pacific tribes used simple geometry to create a design and then twisted it. This Maori diamond shape has been twisted to give the design a much more organic feel, especially when reflected and repeated.